PREFACE

We live in a world today where "political correctness" trumps morals and basic common sense. God's children know that Satan is the prince of this world and he is having a field day with many people. Like the Bible warns us, in the end times evil will be considered good and good evil. We are seeing this prophecy already playing out. God is still in control and when He has had enough, He will bring an end to it. In the meantime, the children of God (blood bought children through Jesus Christ) must stand for God. He does not change. His Word, His precepts, His commands, are as applicable today as they were 3,000 plus years ago. We must stand for Him, no matter the cost; not with man, not with man's laws that go against God's Law, not with the "politically correct deceivers". If we want the true liberty that we can have through Jesus Christ, we must be willing to go against the status quo.

All Scripture comes from the King James Version unless otherwise noted.

Being Sons and Daughters of Liberty
The Bible's Perspective - The Truth

In the perilous times in which we live, it is even more important that God's children know and understand God's Word and recognize that He is the one who gives us freedom and liberty, and His is the Supreme Law of the land. We must understand what that freedom and liberty is, how it relates to our everyday lives, and be ready to defend it even to the point of civil disobedience, no matter the cost to our person.

Read Luke 14:28-33 - What does Jesus say here about counting the cost?

Luke 14:34&35 says (KJV) "Salt is good: but if the salt have lost his savour, wherewith shall it be seasoned? It is neither fit for the land, nor yet for the dunghill; but men cast it out. He that hath ears to hear, let him hear."

According to, **The New Strongs Expanded Exhaustive Concordance of the Bible** (2001 [Greek] Pg. 169 §3471) "when salt is damp it clumps and loses its properties, much like when believers 'clump' and fail to give thirst to the world for Christ and fail to stop its ever-encroaching evil". We are in a battle now to stop this ever-encroaching evil in our nation, but we must have the savour (the oomph, the kick, the flavor) of Jesus Christ to do so. Take notice what Jesus says in **Verse 35** about salt that has lost its savour. It is not fit for the land nor even a dunghill.

We all know what a dunghill is. He goes on to say that when this happens, men throw it out.

What do you think God does when this happens?

The statement, "He that hath ears to hear, let him hear", is very important. When Jesus makes this statement, He means what He has said before is very important, and we better pay attention.

This study is going to focus on what it means to the children of God to be a son or daughter of liberty; what does God say about it; and what are our rights, privileges, and responsibilities as such.

The Oxford English Dictionary defines liberty as:

"the state of being free within society from oppressive restrictions imposed by authority on one's way of life, behavior, or political views":

synonyms: independence · freedom · autonomy · sovereignty · self-government · self-rule · self-determination · civil liberties · human rights

The Greek word for liberty in the noun sense is eleutheria (el-yoo-ther-ee-ah); in the liberty where Christ has made us free; freedom; freedom from bondage. **The New Strongs Expanded Exhaustive Concordance of the Bible** (2001 [Greek] Pg. 84 §1657)

See Galatians 5:1

Also in the adjective sense, the word is eleutheros (el-yoo-ther-os) (as a citizen) unrestrained, to go at pleasure, not as a slave, exempt from obligation or liability, freedom to go wherever one likes. **ibid §1658**

God is sovereign. That means that He is the Supreme Power over everything. He created everything, He is in control of everything, nothing exists without His say so; so He is the Supreme Ruler over this nation, this world, this universe and all of the heavens. If we are a child of God, and believe that to be true; then we should never adhere to any manmade rule, law, or doctrine that conflicts with God's.

His sovereignty means that all nations of the world are subject to Him. The President of the United States is subject to God. You might say well he doesn't obey God. That might be true but it does not take away the fact that God is His Boss whether or not He chooses to obey Him. **See Romans 14:11&12, Philippians 2:9-11 & II Chronicles 20:6**

Governments and leaders of nations are not exempted from obeying God's laws.

See Psalms 115:3

God does not change, His laws/commands do not change. Just because a society or a government decides to make their own laws, or a church denomination decides to add their own doctrine; does not change the laws and

4

commands of God.   His always supercedes any others. **See Malachi 3:6a.**

So, where does that leave God's children today in the unholy, evil nation and world in which we live? We will see what the Scriptures say.

The Declaration of Independence which was put into effect July 4, 1776, recognized God's laws and based its contents on the same.   **"We hold these truths to be self-evident, that all men are created equal, that they are endowed by their Creator with certain unalienable Rights, that among these are Life, Liberty, and the pursuit of Happiness —That to secure these rights, Governments, are instituted among Men, deriving their just powers from the consent of the governed, — That whenever any Form of Government becomes destructive of these ends, it is the Right of the People to alter or to abolish it, and to institute new Government."**

God's children have a duty to disregard, disobey any law that is in conflict with God's laws and commands. **See Acts 5:29**

What is civil disobedience? *Merriam Webster's definition is:*

> "refusal to obey governmental demands or commands especially as a nonviolent and usually collective means of forcing concessions from the government"

In the spiritual sense, civil disobedience would be God's children refusing to obey a law or laws, rules or regulations, that go against God's laws and or commands.

While we are going through this study, let's keep in mind Amendment I of the Constitution which is part of the Bill of Rights:

> **"Congress shall make no law respecting an establishment of religion, or prohibiting the free exercise thereof; or abridging the freedom of speech, or of the press, or the right of the people peaceably to assemble, and to petition the government for redress of grievances."**

And also Amendment 10 which is part of the Bill of Rights:

> **"The powers not delegated to the United States by the Constitution, nor prohibited by it to the States, are reserved to the States respectively, or to the people."**

What laws are on the books now that violate God's laws?

1. **Same-Sex Marriage** - On June 26, 2015, a previous case was overturned by the Supreme Court as a result of *Obergefell v Hodges,* the ruling stated that states could no longer have a ban on same-sex marriage. Up to this time 13 states were still holding out. The Supreme Court stated that this issue fell

under the Fourteenth Amendment of the Constitution in reference to due process and equal protection.

The United States Code is a multi-volume publication of text of statutes enacted by Congress. As of January 3, 2012, and no update since then as far as I can see, marriage is defined as:

"Definition of 'marriage' and 'spouse'

In determining the meaning of any Act of Congress, or of any ruling, regulation, or interpretation of the various administrative bureaus and agencies of the United States, the word 'marriage' means only a legal union between one man and one woman as husband and wife, and the word 'spouse' refers only to a person of the opposite sex who is a husband or a wife. 1 US Code, Title 1, Chapter 1, §7

As of June 17, 2017, this definition was still in effect. **So, what does this say about the Supreme Court decision in** *Obergefell v Hodges*? **Also, did this ruling violate states' rights?**

You might say what does this have to do with me. "I don't have to recognize it or agree with it. Let them do what they want." It might not affect you directly right now, but it does indirectly.

Case in Point - Kim Davis - County Clerk in Kentucky who refused to issue marriage licenses to gay couples saying she was acting under God's authority. She ended up being jailed for contempt of court for still refusing to issue the licenses after the court ordered her to do so.

What is your take on this? Do you agree with her or would you have gone ahead and issued the licenses?

The case ended by the new governor issuing an executive order which stated that marriage licenses do not have to have the clerk's name on them. In so doing, Ms. Davis did not have to issue the licenses to gay couples, nor was her name on the licenses. The deputy clerks now issue those licenses. God always defends His children when they refuse to compromise. They may have to suffer some persecution and trials along the way, but He will never forsake them.

What do you think about your clerks, ones that claim to be Christians, issuing these licenses?

Case #2 - Colorado couple who refused to bake a wedding cake for a gay couple. This couple refused on the basis that it violated their religious beliefs. They stood their ground, the court ruled against them, and they had to close their doors. A similar case happened in Oregon. The owners were ruled against and were ordered to pay the gay couple up to $150,000 in damages. More such cases have since occurred.

Do you believe these cases are protected under the First Amendment?

Since the Supreme Court decision in *Obergefell v Hodges* stated that states can no longer have a ban on same-sex marriage, with no other specifics, the door is left open for states to require pastors to perform such marriages.

What should be a pastor's response if asked to do so knowing that refusing to do so would mean breaking state law?

What does God say about same-sex marriage? List some scriptures to back up your answer.

2. Home Bible Studies - There are actually some cities across the country that have banned home Bible Studies and/or require a permit to have one. A catholic group in San Capistrano, California was fined $300 for holding a home Bible Study. The city of Rancho Cucamonga, California says that a group must have a permit to hold a home Bible Study. There has been more than one city in Arizona that has put a ban on home Bible Studies. A Pastor in Phoenix, Arizona was fined $12,000 and spent 60 days in jail for refusing to stop having Bible Studies on his property. A couple in Venice, Florida was fined for not having a permit to have a Bible Study in their home and was also fined for having a pray sign in their yard, was told it was against zoning laws.

Once again we can see these types of cases as violations of our First Amendment rights. Also, part of the Fifth Amendment states, "No person...nor be deprived of life, liberty, or property, without due process of law". Well you might say that the city made the law so you have to abide by it. However, according to the Tenth Amendment, States cannot make any law that is in conflict with the rights guaranteed under the Constitution. These types of laws are in violation of the First Amendment. Remember the First Amendment says that Congress shall make no law that would forbid the right of the people peaceably to assemble.

Taking all of this into consideration, what would be God's response to this kind of prohibition? Give some Scriptures.

3. <u>**Abortion**</u> - In 1973, the Supreme Court ruled in *Roe v Wade*:

"Yes. State criminal abortion laws that except from criminality only life-saving procedures on the mother's behalf, and that do not take into consideration the stage of pregnancy and other interests, are unconstitutional for violating the Due Process Clause of the Fourteenth Amendment."

"Yes. The Due Process Clause protects the right to privacy, including a woman's right to terminate her pregnancy, against state action."

The Supreme Court stated that abortion restrictions were in violation of the due process clause of the Fourteenth Amendment and went further to say that the due process clause protects the right to privacy. So what happened to the right to privacy and use of your private property for home Bible Studies? What has happened to due process for Christians to not have their beliefs violated under the First Amendment?

What happened to due process for the unborn child? It is a living being.

According to Oxford Dictionaries, the definition of due process is: "fair treatment through the normal judicial system, especially as a citizen's entitlement".

SB1564 in Illinois was signed by Governor Rauner. This bill forces pro-life doctors who will not perform abortions to either: refer the patient to another provider they think will provide the services, transfer the patient to another provider who they think will provide the services, or provide the patient with a list of providers they believe will provide the services.

What do you believe a Christian doctor should do? Do you think his/her obeying this law would constitute him supporting abortion?

What does God say about abortion? Give some scriptures.

4. The right of the people to keep and bear arms

The Second Amendment of the US Constitution says, "... the right of the people to keep and bear Arms, shall not be infringed." The definition of the word bear in the verb sense means to carry (Oxford Dictionaries). Many states are in violation of this amendment. As we have mentioned before, the Tenth Amendment gives the states powers that are not delegated by the Constitution and are not prohibited by it. So, the United States Constitution has already given its citizens the right to carry arms; guns, swords, knives, whatever. Carry means on the person. States forbidding altogether or putting restrictions on the carry violate the United States Constitution; and if you want to take it a step further as the United States Supreme Court has ruled in other cases, violates due process. Forty-five states allow open carry of firearms, fifteen of these require permits. Concealed carry is a whole other issue. Let's just look at Illinois. Open carry is not allowed, and in order to get a concealed carry permit, you first have to have a FOID (Firearms Owner ID) card to even purchase firearms and ammo; go through a multi-hour class which on the average costs around $300. Part of the class is being able to hit specific targets within three different distance ranges and you must have at least 80% on each one. Then, if you make it through all that, you have to pay numerous fees to apply for the permit and fingerprinting; and then your medical records are checked and your local police department is contacted to see if they have any reason as to why you should not have a permit. To top it all off, Illinois does not recognize any other states' permits. As a result, some states will not recognize Illinois' permits since they won't recognize theirs. All of these kinds of prohibitions and restrictions to try to keep citizens from bearing arms is in direct violation of our rights under the Second Amendment of the United States Constitution, and the states are violating the Tenth Amendment.

Are there any Scriptures supporting bearing arms? If so what are they?

5. Transgender Issues

Now there is a lot of hullabaloo about transgender issues. **Genesis 5:2(a) [this is God speaking] says,**

14

"Male and female created he them..." I don't think I need to say anything else about this subject. The Word speaks for itself.

BIBLICAL HISTORY OF GOVERNMENT

Let's back up and see how all this government came about with man's laws. Before the Mosaic Law, man pretty much did what they felt was right in their own eyes. However, God communed with His children and they were aware of what was right and what was wrong. He made Adam and Eve aware of sin. He made Cain aware of his sin. Noah was aware of what the sin was in his land. God chose people like Abraham to lead His people and instill in them right from wrong.

What does Romans 2:14&15 say about this? See also Romans 1:20:

Then Moses came along and God gave him the Ten Commandments along with the Mosaic Law which set down specifics on ordinances and the worship system. Now the people were really made aware of how sinful they were. Under the Mosaic Law Judges were appointed to handle disputes. This system sufficed for about 450 years until the people decided they needed a human king.

See I Samuel 8:1-7 - What is God's response and what is the problem?

See also Acts 13:17-21

God chose Saul. He started out good, but the power went to his head. God removed his anointing, and he was destroyed. David was a man after God's own heart, but he had issues also; Solomon messed up; and on and on. If you look at the history of the kings of Israel; for the most part, not a pretty picture. Anytime you put man in control of something without God in the equation, you have a recipe for disaster.

There are differences in opinions from scholars and Christian theologians on just how Christian is our Constitution. No matter how you look at the Constitution, you have to remember that it was written by men, not the Holy inspired Word of God - the Bible; and it is fallible. Granted, I think the framers had good, moral intentions, and many of them were guided by God; but as we can see today, man has eschewed it; see it as an outdated document; and have in many cases totally violated it - man's way of twisting things to fit their purposes. As Christians, God's children through the blood of Jesus Christ, our plumbline must always be the Word of God; not the Constitution, not national and local laws, not politically correct leaders. If it does not measure up to God's law, then we are not to abide by it.

According to some sources, at least 50 of the 55 framers of the U.S. Constitution were Christians (see M. E. Bradford's book, "A Worthy Company; Brief Lives of the Framers of the United States Constitution"). As children of God, we know that some people have a very loose definition of the term Christian. However, we do know that the Constitution contains many concepts that are based on Biblical principles.

The argument against the Constitution by some scholars is that colonial American government before the Constitution's ratification was based on God's law instead of man's laws; citing that the Constitution places priority on the will of the people and not that of God's; i.e., "we the people of the United States..." (Preamble to the Constitution). In an article entitled "Bible Law vs. the United States Constitution", posted on missiontoisrael.org, are listed eight Biblical infractions:

- The Preamble's substitution of a new national god in place of God
- Article1's usurpation of God's legislative powers
- Article 2's commandeering of God's executive sovereignty
- Article 3's supplanting of God's judicial system

- Article 6's repudiation of Christianity
- Amendment 1's promotion of pluralism, polytheism, and idolatry
- Amendment 2's replacement of the Biblical responsibility to bear arms
- Amendment 8's condemnation of God's judgments

Take a look at the United States Constitution. **Do you agree with these bullet points? Why or why not?**

This study is not to dis the Constitution but rather to make you think about how it applies to your walk with God. There are some good protections in there for us, the problem is that it is being disregarded in many cases; misinterpreted and maligned. It is our responsibility as Christians to always assess governments and their laws in relation to God's laws, and act accordingly.

GOD'S SOVEREIGNTY

What does sovereignty mean?

Exodus 20:3 - How does this verse apply here?

See Psalms 83:18; Isaiah 9:6&7; Acts 17:24&25

What other scriptures talk about God's sovereignty?

God's law is the Supreme Law of the universe. The United States Constitution makes no reference to His authority in the preamble or in the religious clauses. The word God is mentioned in the preamble of eight states' constitutions; term Supreme Ruler of the Universe in four states; term Almighty God in 30 states. Some states' constitutions have no preamble, but divine references are made in other places in their constitutions. Oregon is the only state that has a preamble that does not mention God, but uses the term Almighty God in its religious clauses.

ABSOLUTE TRUTHS

Absolute means that it is not up for question, it has total power and authority. Even some so-called theologians will say that some things in the Bible cannot be taken as absolute. God does not deal in maybes, and He does not change with time.

What Bible verse(s) tells us that God does not change?

God has fixed standards. There is an absolute existence of moral standards according to God's law. The Declaration of Independence makes reference to such : "We hold these truths to be self-evident...endowed by their Creator with certain unalienable rights...".

See Exodus 20:1-17; Psalms 119:142,152

RULE OF GOD'S LAW RATHER THAN THE AUTHORITY OF MAN

See Isaiah 8:19&20; Matthew 5:17&18

ALL MEN ARE SINNERS

There were checks and balances built into the Constitution because the framers realized that men are sinners and there needed to be oversight on each other. That is why the three branches of the government were established. However, as we know, this oversight has not been enough for corrupt government not to override these checks and balances and do what they want. Presidents have overstepped their authority and issued orders without consulting the legislative branch. The judicial branch has gotten into the business at times of making law rather than interpreting it. Making laws are supposed to be under the jurisdiction of the legislative branch - on, and on, and on.

See Genesis 1:26 - What happened though?

1 John 1:8; Genesis 8:21; Jeremiah 17:9

ALL MEN ARE CREATED EQUAL

This phrase is stated in the Declaration of Independence.

What is the key word in this phrase and how are the results altered?

See Acts 10:34; Acts 17:26; Galatians 3:28

THREE BRANCHES OF GOVERNMENT

See Isaiah 33:22

The three branches cannot be said to be based upon this Scripture, **what has become the problem?**

RELIGIOUS FREEDOM

First Amendment - "Congress shall make no law respecting an establishment of religion, or prohibiting the free exercise thereof"...

Do we have free exercise today? Explain your answer.

See I Timothy 2:1&2

FREEDOM OF SPEECH

Our freedom of speech is supposed to be guaranteed by Amendment I of the Constitution. However, it seems today that certain groups' rights to freedom of speech are being upheld and others not. The LBGT community can spew all kinds of hateful rhetoric against the Christian community and it has been deemed free speech; but if Christians want to voice their views, they are hate mongering, even to the point of being classified by some as terrorists. Burning the

American flag has been deemed as freedom of speech, but flying a confederate flag is racist. The liberal media and far left liberals can spew their hate language, and it is freedom of speech; but if the conservative population expresses their views that are in conflict with the left, it is racist, discriminatory - and on and on. It seems some think freedom of speech only applies to a select few. They want to spew their lies and hate, but can't take the heat when someone disagrees with them.

CHURCH PROTECTED FROM GOVERNMENT CONTROL

First Amendment - However, according to God's Word the church is to influence the government. **Deuteronomy 17:18-20; I Kings 3:28**

Do we see this in our government today?

Matthew 14:3&4; Luke 11:52; Acts 4:26-29

In the Old Testament the priests had a lot of influence on the kings. Even in the New Testament when Israel was

24

under Roman rule, the Romans pretty much let the Priests run things as long as they payed their taxes.

REPUBLIC FORM OF GOVERNMENT

A republic form of government is basically one where people are chosen by the people to be the governing body. In modern day, these people are elected. The United States is a Republic. The framers intended for Godly, moral men to govern. The Constitution establishes a Republic. The framers definitely did not want the new America to ever go back under a tyranny type rule from which they had just escaped in Great Britain.

Before the Israelite people demanded a King, God's choice was a Republic type of government; however the governing bodies were chosen by Godly people. It was not a Democracy, left open to the whims of the people.

See Exodus 18:21; Deuteronomy 1:13; Judges 8:22&23; Proverbs 11:14&24:6

What changed after Israel demanded a King?

SELF-GOVERNING

Self-Governing should begin at home. Neither the Federal or the State government has a right to come into our homes and tell us how to raise our families. The First, Second, Ninth, and Tenth Amendments protect these rights. Our Self-Governing is to be based on God's Law. **Galatians 5:18; I Corinthians 6:1-8; I Timothy 3:1-5; Titus 2:1-8**

Where has government encroached upon this protection?

FAIR TRIAL WITH WITNESSES

Protected by the Sixth Amendment

Deuteronomy 19:15; Proverbs 24:28; Matthew 18:16

When should Christians go to the world court system?

PRIVATE PROPERTY RIGHTS

Protected by the Fifth Amendment

Exodus 20:15-17

There is a loophole in this amendment - **Eminent domain** : the power of government or its agent to take private property for pubic use [it is supposed to benefit the public] with compensation.

Where do you see the abuse of this concept?

A lot of these land grabs are by big developers. They get local government in their pockets. The local government sees dollar signs in taxes and the developer makes millions for hotels, malls, ball stadiums, etc. - not a necessity for the general public good. The landowner who is forced to let the property go, gets a one time payment which usually does not compensate for a lifetime income lost. **One such case happened to a man in Florida. His businesses and land were taken to put up a stadium and a hotel. He lost** money because he tried to fight it and had to pay off a lot of attorney fees.

Do you think this was the original intent for the fifth amendment? Do you see this as stealing in relation to the Exodus 20:15-17 Scripture?

BIBLICAL LIBERTY/FREE ENTERPRISE

Noted in Declaration of Independence - pursuit of happiness.

Free enterprise is an economic system where private business operates in competition, mainly free of state control (Oxford Dictionary). The key word here is "mainly". The United States' free enterprise system operates on five main principles: *freedom to choose your business; right to private property; profit motive; competition; consumer sovereignty.* www.socialstudieshelp.com

Do you see where any of these principles are infringed upon?

Is our Biblical liberty violated? What about the bakery people?

John 8:36; II Corinthians 3:17; Galatians 5:1

CREATION

Recognized in the Declaration of Independence

Genesis 1:1

CAPITALISM

"an economic and political system in which a country's trade and industry are controlled by private owners for profit, rather than by the state". (Oxford Dictionary)

Liberals have decried our system of capitalism which has made this country great. In recent years our country has been pushing toward Socialism ("a way of organizing a society in which major industries are owned and controlled by the government rather than by individual people and companies") [Merriam Webster Dictionary]. How our society has moved into a form of socialism is the welfare system - some people work their tails off and have to pay for others that do nothing. In a true socialist system, same thing happens. You work for government owned businesses that divvy out, supposedly in equal shares to all, whether or not the workers put in the same effort. This type of system is in violation of the Declaration of Independence and the Constitution.

Biblical Capitalism - Exodus 20:17; Matthew 25:14-30; II Thessalonians 3:6-15;

Anti-trust laws have been enacted, supposedly to protect free enterprise; to keep large businesses from becoming monopolies; thus hindering competition, and to protect small business.

Do you see monopolies in the Bible? If so, what?

Do you agree with the reasoning behind the anti-trust laws and do you think they violate God's principles?

There are other laws within states that are based on biblical principles. These that I have noted are referenced either directly or indirectly in the United States Constitution and/or the Declaration of Independence.

When the early settlers came to the United States, it was mostly to escape tyranny, to be able to worship their God freely. Most of them were a God-fearing people. The society that the framers lived in was a God-fearing society. The United States Constitution and the Declaration of Independence were instituted with God in mind. The problem is not with the documents themselves, but with the people. Over the centuries man's lust for power, sin, has tarnished these documents; violated them and the peoples' rights that they are to protect. And, first and foremost, God has been taken out of the equation. When God is taken out of the equation, then rights and rules are defined by whomever has the most power.

Government is to prevent evil. **Romans 13:1-5; I Peter 2:13-17**

Is our government today preventing evil?

John Adams said, "We have no government armed with power capable of contending with human passions unbridled by morality and religion. Avarice, ambition, revenge, or gallantry, would break the strongest cords of our Constitution as a whale goes through a net. Our Constitution was made only for a moral and religious people. It is wholly inadequate to the government of any other."

As stated on *faithfacts.org*, the first most important level of government is self-government; and as John Adams stated, that is why religion must be encouraged. The second most important level of government is the family; the third is the church, and lastly is civil government.

Would this hierarchy be possible in our society today? Why or why not?

That brings us down to civil government. As the Scriptures in Romans 13:1-5 and I Peter 2:13-17 state, the purpose of civil government is to restrain evil and reward good.

What does I Timothy 2:1-4 tell us? What is the exception to obeying the government?

No government exists without God allowing it to do so. That does not necessarily mean that He approves of it. We have freewill and He allows us to make choices, and we suffer the consequences of those choices.

Christians are to take part in government issues to influence the government for God, and remind it that all is under His authority. **Psalms 24:1; Psalms 83:18; Isaiah 42:8; Matthew 28:18-20; II Corinthians 10:5**

CIVIL DISOBEDIENCE

Civil Disobedience is going against your government.

In God's eyes, when is this acceptable?

Examples of Civil Disobedience in the Bible:

Acts 5:28&29; Acts 4:18-20; Daniel 3:1-30; Exodus 1:15-22; Daniel 6:1-28; Acts 5:40-42; Romans 12:2; Acts 16:37; Joshua 2:1-7; Luke 12:47; I Kings 18:3&4; I Samuel 14:45; Luke 22:36

Why would they need a sword?

How did Esther show civil disobedience?

In what respect could you possibly see yourself committing civil disobedience in the future? Would you be willing to do so even if it meant loss of your job or business, imprisonment for yourself, or your children or other family members being punished by you doing so?

Did Jesus commit civil disobedience?

Mark 1:14

John 2:14-16 - How was this an act of subversive non-violent civil disobedience?

The Jewish priests ruled over the general population in Jesus' day. They answered to the Roman Government, but they were a government within themselves. As long as tribute was paid to the Romans and there were no uprisings against the Roman government, they left the Jews to rule over their own people within their circle. So, when Jesus came in and announced that He was God and the Messiah, I would say the powers that were felt threatened, which we know they were by the results we see.

Luke 4:17-19 - Jesus is talking about upsetting their whole way of living. The Jewish hierarchy didn't care about the poor. The poor were oppressed and downtrodden. The Pharisees were power hungry, greedy people, who were a bunch of hypocrites. Jesus himself called them hypocrites. **Matthew 23:25&26**

Mark 1:23-26 - Now Jesus is in the temple casting out demons. Did the Pharisees authorize this?

Mark 1:40-45 - Jesus heals the leper. Why would this be an act of disobedience to the authority of the Pharisees? NOTE: Lepers were untouchables, the priests would have nothing to do with them.

Matthew 9:10 - Jesus was a Jew. Jews did not associate with publicans and sinners. In Jewish society two groups were recognized as sinners: those that were recognized criminals, and those that had occupations they considered ro be sinful or unlawful such as a tax collectors. They also considered those who could not follow temple procedures because of sickness or poverty as sinners.

What about all those times Jesus worked and healed on the Sabbath? **Mark 2:23-28**

What other Scripture(s) show Jesus working or healing on the Sabbath?

Mark 7:3 -Not washing your hands before eating in the Jewish culture was considered to be a breaking of the Jewish law which would result in condemnation and excommunication. **Luke 11:37-43**

Jesus associated with enemies of the government: Gerasenes, Samaritans, and Greeks. This would have been considered treasonous. Remember the woman at the well - she was a Samaritan. He also healed people in the hated Roman hierarchy. **Luke 7:1-10** There were revolutionaries during this time that were plotting to overthrow the Roman government, so this action would have placed Jesus on the wrong side.

Do you think Pastors/Teachers/Evangelists should preach and teach things that are contrary to the law of the land? Why/why not?

It was very common in the seventeenth and eighteenth centuries for preachers to speak out against the government. "No idea was more fully stressed, no principle more often repeated, through the first sixty years of the eighteenth century, than that governments must obey law and that he who resisted one in authority who was violating that law was not himself a rebel but a protector of law" (*The New England Pulpit and the American Revolution* by Alice M. Baldwin, out of the forword by Joel McDurmon) Preachers routinely preached civil disobedience and armed resistance when necessary. When people were trying to garner power and tried to enforce wicked laws, they were confronted by an army of parishioners led by preachers.

Why does this not happen today?

Our government is bound by the same laws as the citizens, so when it does not obey, it is acting illegally.

The early Americans believed that a government which did not have the good of the people at heart was not sanctioned by God; that people have natural rights, inalienable rights (those given by God) and no government had the right to infringe upon those rights. They chose governments that were not in conflict with God's laws. "All lawful authority comes from God and must be obeyed, but unlawful and usurped authority may be resisted". (*Will and Doom*, by G. Bulkeley)

> "Where executive and legislative authority exceed the bounds of the law of God and the constitution, then their acts are ipso facto (by that very fact) void" (*op.cit.* Pg 127)

An example of one of the most violent articles written during this time was written by the preacher John Cleaveland of Ipswich against General Gage. On June 17, 1775, he wrote,

> "Thou profane, wicked-monster of falsehood and perfidy...your late infamous proclamation is as full of notorious lies, as a toad or rattle-snake of deadly poison—you are an abandoned wretch...Without speedy repentance, you will have an aggravated damnation in hell...you are not only a robber, a murderer, and usurper, but a wicked Rebel: A rebel

against the authority of truth, law, equity, the English constitution of government, these colony states, and humanity itself." (*Essex Gazette)*

A young preacher, Joseph Lyman, from Lebanon, Connecticut, in 1772 preached Sunday after Sunday, as well as in town meetings, the doctrine of liberty and resistance.

A surprising number of preachers served in the Revolutionary War. These were a people that believed that God ruled over men by a divine constitution, and that noone was obligated to obey an unconstitutional act. They also believed that when a government was operating illegally, not obeying the laws; then with consent of the people, they had a right to abolish that government and establish a new one. They believed that religious liberty and civil liberty must work together; that one could not be separated from the other.

E. Pemberton, *On the Power and Limitations of Magistrates, Massachusetts Election Sermon,* 1710:

> "The Power of the greatest Potentate on Earth is not Inherent in him, but is a Derivative...For God is the Source and Original of all Power; there is no Power but what is derived from him, depends on him, is limited by him, and is subordinate to him, and accountable... Rulers are to be the Guardians of their Peoples' Religion and Property, their Liberties, Civil & Sacred..."

As stated in Dutch Sheets' book, *An Appeal to Heaven,* he states,

> "The original American Dream wasn't about wealth, but freedom—freedom to worship and freedom from tyranny." "But America has perverted this holy desire and God-honoring partnership, turning the dream into a narcissistic lust for money, possessions and pleasure." "Liberty became license; independence became rebellion; and our'freedoms' enslaved us." "And we are no longer feeding on the dream; the dream is feeding on us."

So, you get the point here. This was a time of great revolutionaries that helped to make the United States a great nation by the grace of God. This nation has become so degenerate that I can't even imagine what the framers or some of these great men of God would think. There have been revivals in our nation's history since then that have awakened some of the people for a while, but once again the nation is asleep; many Christians are asleep. Is God going to give us one last revival before He comes back? He will, but it requires the commitment, work, and sacrifice of His people humbling themselves before Him.

Are you committed enough, strong enough in your walk with the Lord, to commit civil disobedience against your government if necessary?

Remember Matthew 10:33 - If you place your government over God, then you are denying Him. You have to choose which master you will serve. **Matthew 6:24** You cannot ride the fence. God will not accept that. **James 1:8; Revelation 3:16**

AFTERWORD

This book has been put together as a Bible Study, to challenge Christians to stand for God, to understand that God should always be at the top of their pyramid; above family, above government. This study, whether used in a group setting or on a personal level, should make you child of God think about the what ifs. What would you do? And, to you non-believers, it should serve as a warning. You can see I have included many questions that will require you to dig deep into yourself, and also into the Bible to find applicable Scriptures. However, I am going to summarize a few of the issues I have previously put out there for you to discuss and decide.

Same-Sex marriage (Homosexuality) - It is an abomination (God hates it) to the Lord. **See Leviticus 18:22.** And if you are thinking that this is Old Testament Scripture and not applicable, look at **I Corinthians 6:9-11**. I hope you found the other Old Testament and New Testament Scriptures that deal with this subject. It is not a disease, it is a choice. There is nowhere in the Bible where God condemns a disease, He does condemn bad choices (sin).

Preaching and Teaching God's Word - There may come a time, if you live long enough, that you will be told not to preach or teach, or even mention God's Word; with the threat of severe punishment or loss of life. There are parts of the world where people are already experiencing this type of persecution. What stance will you take? God the Son is very clear in His Word that if you deny Him before men, He will deny you before the Father.

Abortion - I hope **Jeremiah 1:5** is one of the Scriptures you found relative to this subject. I don't think any other explanation is needed here.

Right to Keep and Bear Arms - There are Scriptures to back up this statement. If you did not find them, go back and look again.

All Men Are Created Equal - The key word is created. They are all created equal, but they don't all end up equal based on their freewill choices. Some go to spend eternity in Hell and some go to spend eternity in Heaven with the Lord. God does not send them to hell, they send themselves to hell for refusing to surrender their lives to Jesus Christ.

Obeying Your Government - I hope you answered that there may come a time when you have to disobey your government, and it will be acceptable. That time will come when your government tells you to do something that goes against the Word of God. Some are already having to make those decisions. **Remember God is the Supreme Authority**.

www.ingramcontent.com/pod-product-compliance
Lightning Source LLC
Chambersburg PA
CBHW071144280526
45787CB00003B/1399